The Architect of After

From the Red Dirt of Jamaica to the Office of Success

NALHLIE DALY, HON. DR.

Foreword by: The Honorable Judge Stephen N. Knights, Jr.

Cover art/illustrator by: Candice Messado

Editor: Nicole Palmer of Nicole Williams Collective

An imprint of Living By The Daly Standard, LLC

ISBN: 979-8-9960869-0-0 (paperback)

ISBN: 979-8-9960869-1-7 (Kindle/ebook)

Library of Congress Control Number: 2026912391

Printed in the United States of America

Praise for *The Architect of After*

"*The Architect of After: From the Red Dirt of Jamaica to the Office of Success* is both powerful and deeply inspiring—a work that speaks to the heart while challenging the mind. The author writes with authenticity, wisdom, and a clear sense of purpose, making every page impactful and memorable. It's not just a book you read; it's one you experience. A truly remarkable contribution from a gifted and insightful voice of a Life Coach, Dr. Nalhlie Daly.

This book is a powerful vessel of truth, hope, and transformation. The author writes with spiritual depth and clarity, guiding readers into a deeper understanding of purpose and faith. Every chapter carries wisdom that not only inspires but calls you higher. This is more than a book—it's a divine encounter through the written word."

— ***Dr. Chris Scott****, Pastor, Church Beyond Walls Outreach Ministries & Master Life Coach*

DEDICATION

To Candice,

You were the passenger in the backseat when the rain hit the roof.

You were the reason I kept walking when the three buses felt like a thousand miles.

This book is your inheritance—not of my pain, but of my resilience.

Always remember: you are not the dirt; you are the harvest.

I am so proud to be the Architect, because it led me to being your mother.

TABLE OF CONTENTS

FOREWORD

By: The Honorable Judge Stephen N. Knights, Jr.

Throughout my years on the bench, I saw thousands of people in the courtroom and looked each of them in their eyes during the proceedings. I often learn about parts of a person's life that led them to being in court. Those circumstances may vary. But what is constant is that I remain fair and impartial, secure the rights of all, and serve with compassion, humility, and humanity. I follow the black letter of the law and give hope — through conversation and encouragement — to let individuals know that a moment in court does not solely define their next steps in life. What is key is that a person can put whatever happened behind them and ultimately move forward once the court proceedings and after-court events have ended.

In looking into the eyes of many, I sometimes see the heavy weight of defeat in those overwhelmed by their circumstances. At other times, I see the jagged edges of trauma left behind from violence or loss. In a courtroom, it is important that “the record” is clear. The record is what can be reviewed in transcript form — the history of every word spoken and everything that happened. In life, a record may be a static history of events, a ledger of debts, or even a series of verdicts that can sometimes feel final. And yet we know there are times when a person walks into a room and simply refuses to be defined by their past record.

In my role as a Board Member of Leadership Henry, I first met Dr. Nalhlie Daly at the Leadership Henry Class of 2025–2026. At the time, I knew only of her professional reputation in risk assessment, her intellect, and her ability to hone leadership skills. Later, I learned a glimpse into the ‘Red Dust’ from which she emerged. When I read the details of her childhood — the murder of her mother, the ‘Neighborhood Ghost’ of her father, the eight-mile walks in hand-sewn skirts — I had a profound realization: Dr. Nalhlie Daly is a woman who refused to be defined by the record, and who refused to let poverty or pain write the final chapter of her life.

We know that a structural engineer or architect creates calculations and blueprints to ensure a structure can withstand storms. In these pages, Dr. Nalhlie Daly reveals how she became the Architect of her own life. She does not simply tell a story of survival — she provides the engineering specs for how she moved from being a "beggar scholar" in Jamaica to an Honorary Doctor and an Executive in America.

The Architect of After is an honest journey. Dr. Nalhlie Daly does not shy away from the 'Jamaican Knot' — that tight, bitter, ball of resentment carried by someone who knows profound unfairness. She shows that the red dirt others may mistake for a grave is actually the nutrient-rich soil intended for your planting. This shift in mindset is the manual for anyone standing in the rubble of their own life — whether from a literal hurricane, a health crisis, or the quiet, steady erosion of their dreams.

The Architect of After is the testimony of a woman who jumped from a moving car to protect her future, who changed clothes in the darkness of homeless nights, and who ultimately claimed the seat she spent a lifetime earning. Dr. Nalhlie Daly proves that the verdict of your past does not always define you. The future is yours to build.

ACKNOWLEDGMENT

A Tribute to the Pillar

To My Husband, Donovan

There are pillars that hold up buildings, and then there are the pillars that hold up a soul. Donovan, you have been the unyielding foundation upon which I have built my 'After.'

Writing this book required me to travel back—emotionally, spiritually, and sometimes physically—into the red dust and the shadows of 1981, into places I had sealed away for decades and was not sure I had the strength to revisit.

Thank you for your relentless support. For holding my hand when the memories became too heavy. For being the steady, quiet strength that gave me the safety to find my voice and the courage to use it.

You never once doubted the Architect, even when the blueprints were blurred by tears. You showed up in the smallest, most essential ways—and in doing so, you showed me what true partnership looks like when it is stripped of performance and filled with purpose.

You are the silent partner in every victory and the peace in every storm. This work, and the woman I am today, would not be complete without your love.

Thank you for standing by me. Thank you for believing in the mission. Thank you for proving, every single day, that the greatest sanctuary of all is a love that does not waver.

###

INTRODUCTION
The Blueprint of a Life

The first thing people notice about me today is my confidence. It is a polished, practiced stillness—the kind that is not inherited but earned, one hard mile at a time. They see the silver emblem on the hood of my Mercedes-Benz catching the morning sun. They see the crisp, sharp lines of my tailored blazer, the heavy weight of a doctoral hood in the photographs on my office wall, and the rows of degrees and professional designations framed beside them. To my coaching clients, I am "The Architect"—the woman who builds ironclad boundaries and helps others engineer their best lives. They assume the road was always paved for me.

They don't know about the red dust.

They don't know that for seventeen years, I could not say the word 'Mother' without a bitter taste rising in my throat. They don't know about the eight-mile walk through the Jamaican heat, my bare feet toughened like leather, or the terrifying price I once paid just to get a ride to a classroom. They don't know that I have been homeless in the land of plenty—dressing for executive meetings in the cramped backseat of a car that held everything I owned in plastic bags, while my eight-year-old daughter slept beside me, trusting me to make it right.

I came to America at twenty-six years old with a suitcase full of books, a head full of dreams, and the grit of a girl who had already survived more than most people twice her age. I came for 'opportunity'. I came to build. And build I did—through grief, through assault, through hurricanes (literal and personal), through single motherhood and graduate school, and a diagnosis that changed the air in the room. I built when I had no blueprint. I built when the walls were still shaking.

This book is that blueprint.

I am writing this for the girl standing on the shoulder of the road, wondering if she will ever be more than a victim. I am writing it for the woman who is dressing for success in the backseat of her car, who has convinced herself that the dirt she is buried in is a grave. I am here to tell you it is not.

You are not the dirt you were buried in. You are the seed.

And it is time for you to rise.

###

CHAPTER ONE
The Hood and the Honor

Standing on that university stage, the doctoral hood felt like a mantle of heavy, noble velvet. It was a deep, saturated color—the kind of hue that demands respect—and its weight was a physical anchor against the dizzying swirl of my emotions. The air in the auditorium was thick with the scent of expensive perfume, floor wax, and the electric hum of over a hundred collective breaths held in anticipation.

The blinding stage lights turned the audience into a sea of shadows. My heart was not just beating; it was a rhythmic drum, echoing the ghosts of every mile I had ever walked. I scanned the darkness, searching for an anchor. Then, the shadows broke. I saw my husband

and daughter in the front row. And behind them – my entire congregation, my community, the people who had watched me walk this long road. And while they had been invited, standing there beneath those blinding lights, looking out at every face that had ever believed in me before I fully believed in myself, it felt less like a planned event and more like a miracle that had simply chosen me.

When the title of 'Honorary Doctorate' was bestowed upon me in September of 2025—an Honorary Doctorate in Humanities, awarded by the Jamaican American International Chamber of Commerce (JAICC) in recognition of a lifetime of community service—something ancient began to loosen inside me. I call it the 'Jamaican Knot.' It was a tight, copper-tasting ball of resentment and grief I had carried in my chest for decades, the residue of a childhood that had asked far too much of a girl far too young.

As the hood settled on my shoulders, I looked past the lights and whispered to the one person who could not be in that room. "Mamma, I forgive you. It was not your fault."

Forgiveness is not a feeling. It is a decision. It is the demolition of an old, crumbling structure so that something taller, something more worthy, can rise in its place. I did not forgive my mother for her sake that night. She was long past needing it. I forgave her for mine—for the woman I was becoming, for the daughter watching from the front row, and for the girl I had once been, standing in the red dust of Jamaica with nothing but her tenacity and a dream.

But I am getting ahead of myself. To understand the honor of that stage, you must first understand the road that led there. And that road begins with loss.

###

End of Chapter Reflection Questions:

Who are you holding responsible for your struggle?

____

____

____

____

____

____

____

How is that blame slowing your growth?

____
____
____
____
____
____
____

What would it free in you to offer forgiveness—not for their sake, but for yours?

____
____
____
____
____
____
____

Architect's Blueprint:

Forgiveness is the demolition of an old, crumbling structure so that a skyscraper can rise in its place.

CHAPTER TWO
The Eclipse

January 19, 1981, was the day the sun went out. It shouldn't have—it was my sister Tulip's birthday, a day that had always carried the warm brightness of celebration.

The classroom was a cacophony of scratching pencils and the rhythmic thud-thud of a fan that did little to move the humid Jamaican air. The smell of chalk dust was everywhere—white and sterile. I sat at my desk, a nine-year-old girl with neatly braided hair and clean socks, feeling the particular pride of a child who had made herself presentable against the odds.

The door creaked open midway through the school day. Our teacher, Mrs. Smith—a woman usually as upright and composed as a ruler—had returned from her lunch break looking as if she had been folded in half. Her eyes found me immediately across the room. "Mena," she called out. The word was loud enough to stop thirty pencils at once. Every pair of eyes turned toward me. I stood up instinctively, sure I was in trouble, even though I had never been in trouble a day in my life. "Yes, Mrs. Smith?"

"They murdered your mother."

The words did not make sense. They arrived in my ears as sounds before they became meaning, and in the space between the sound and the meaning, the vibrant greens I could see through the classroom window bled into gray. I felt myself falling backward, the world rushing away from me, and then a pair of arms caught me. To this day, I do not know who held me up.

That morning had been ordinary. My mother had gone to work as she always did, a server in the Food and Beverage Department at a local hotel. She was expected home around eight o'clock in the evening. When nine o'clock came, and she had not appeared at the bus stop where my siblings usually went to meet her, we went to sleep, assuming she had been delayed. It was not until my eldest sister Margaret took a ride to the workplace the following morning that the truth began to surface. My siblings and I had gone to school as usual. We were sitting on the low concrete wall at the side of the road, waiting for the bus, just as we did every morning—not knowing that by the next afternoon, that wall would become the marker of the worst day of our lives.

The drive home from school that day was a blur of red dust and silence. When I reached the neighborhood, I saw what looked like an ocean of people gathered near that wall. Everyone was peering over the edge. I went and looked over it, too. A woman was lying face down in the dirt below. I recognized her white work uniform immediately—the one she wore every single day. I looked to the right and saw hair and dried blood on the barbed wire strung along the top of the wall. "Why didn't I see it this morning?" I thought, and the thought made no sense, and yet it was the only thought I could hold.

Instead of a scream, something cold and hard crystallized in my chest. I felt a fierce, irrational anger

—not at the men who had taken her life, but at her. She was thirty-one years old. She had allowed this to happen. In the raw, desperate logic of a nine-year-old's grief, I decided that her death was a failure of resilience, and I would not make the same mistake. I vowed then and there that I would never mourn her.

I refused to resent the school or the teacher who had delivered the news so bluntly. Instead, I clung to the classroom like a life raft. It became my anchor, my evidence that the future was still possible if I was willing to reach for it. I would be the resilient one. I would not be buried by this.

What I did not understand then, and would not understand for many years, is that resilience is not the absence of grief. It is the decision to keep building even while your hands are shaking.

###

End of Chapter Reflection Questions:

Sometimes, the place where you are most exposed is the place where you find your greatest strength.

What 'places' are you avoiding because of a painful memory attached to them?

____
____
____
____
____
____

What steps are you willing to take to reframe that memory—to reclaim the space that pain has been occupying?

____
____
____
____
____
____
____

Where in your life have you confused resilience with suppression? What might happen if you allowed yourself to grieve and keep building at the same time?

____
____
____

____

____

____

____

Architect's Blueprint:

Trauma is an eclipse—it hides the sun, but it does not extinguish it.

CHAPTER THREE
The Teen Matriarch

The shift happened in the space of a single heartbeat, in the echo of the classroom announcement. One moment, my eldest sister Margaret was seventeen—a girl with her own dreams, the soft peripheral vision of youth, a future that was still entirely hers to write. The next, the crown of matriarchy was pressed onto her brow, and it was made of thorns.

There was no transition period. No orientation for the soul. She did not get to mourn as a daughter; she had to survive as a commander. At seventeen, her hands should have been light, carrying schoolbooks or the tentative weight of a first love. Instead, they became calloused overnight by the heavy, rhythmic labor of keeping six young lives from drifting out to sea.

She became the roof before she had finished being the foundation.

The trauma of that time was a quiet, domestic war. It lived in the kitchen, in the desperate arithmetic of trying to make a single loaf of bread stretch to fill six hungry bellies. It lived in the steam rising from the cornmeal porridge she stirred before dawn, masking the tears that fell silently into the pot. It lived most heavily in the eyes of our youngest brother, Greg, who was only three years old and had not yet learned the word for the absence he would carry for the rest of his life.

To be a child-mother is to live in a state of permanent hyper-vigilance. Margaret walked through the house with the posture of a woman triple her age, her ears always tuned to the frequency of a sibling's cough or the ominous silence that signals a toddler's mischief. She did not just lose her mother that January. She lost her own girlhood. Every time she washed and cooked and cleaned and scrubbed a floor, a piece of her seventeen-year-old self was buried under the red dirt of necessity.

It was the first 'Theft of After' our family endured.

But she did not crumble. She built. Without blueprints, without proper materials, without anyone older to show her the way, she constructed our survival out of scrap cloth and sheer, jagged will. She held the walls up while they were still shaking. She was the first Architect I ever observed, and she taught me things no classroom ever could.

She taught me that leadership is not the loudest voice in the room. It is the steadiest one. She taught me that love, at its most essential, is not a feeling–it is a practice. A daily, unglamorous, ungrateful practice of showing up when you would rather fall apart.

Sometimes the most beautiful structures are the ones built in the middle of a storm, by a girl who refused to let her family fall.

###

End of Chapter Reflection Questions:

When you look back at the sacrifices made by the women in your life, how does acknowledging their "stolen blooms" change the way you view your own success and the legacy you are building?

____

____

____

____

____

____

____

How have you found the strength to be the 'warmth in a house gone cold' when you yourself were shivering? What does that kind of resilience teach you about the difference between being a victim of circumstance and an architect of survival?

____

____

____

____

____

____

____

Architect's Blueprint:

Bloom where you are planted.

CHAPTER FOUR
The Neighborhood Ghost

My father didn't just lose a wife. He lost his soul to the 'Clear Spirit'—the white rum that turned a man into a phantom.

He had been working in the United States government work program when my mother was killed. The authorities contacted him immediately, and he was flown home to attend to her remains and his six children. He arrived devastated—and then he disappeared, not physically, but in every way that mattered. He didn't attend her funeral. He turned instead to the bottle, and the bottle swallowed him whole.

In a small Jamaican neighborhood, shame travels faster than a tropical breeze. My father became what everyone quietly called the 'Neighborhood Ghost'—a man who slept at the side of the road, a man whose presence was an absence. I would be walking home from school laughing with my friends, my uniform clean and pressed, carrying my pride like an invisible accessory, and I would hear the slurred voice cutting through the afternoon heat: "Mena! Mena, it's me!"

The laughter of the other children around me was salt in an open wound. I learned to look through him. I learned to cross the street, to find sudden interest in a stone on the ground, to perform a deafness that I did not feel. What I actually felt was the shattering recognition that my shield had become a ghost. And if he were gone, I would have to be my own father.

That decision—quiet, resolute, made in the glare of a Jamaican afternoon—was one of the most defining of my life. Not because it was right, but because it was necessary. I could not wait for him to become who I needed him to be. I had to become who I needed to be, with or without him.

Things gradually improved after I left that school and moved on to high school. My father and I never spoke of those years. In our culture, to confront a parent was to disrespect them, and so the silence sat between us like heavy furniture—permanent, unacknowledged, impossible to move around. I made my peace with it in my own way, though: I stayed far from alcohol. To this day, the sharp smell of strong spirits carries me back to that road, to that voice, to that man I once called my father. It is a reminder of what unchecked pain can do to a person—and a vow to never let my own pain drive me to disappear.

###

End of Chapter Reflection Questions:

Resilience is the art of fathering your own dreams.

What 'ghosts' of your past are you still trying to outrun? How has the early need to create your own safety shaped who you are today?

Have you experienced an internal struggle rooted in unspoken trauma? What did it cost you to carry it silently—and what might it free in you to finally speak it?

Architect's Blueprint:

You cannot wait for your parents to become who you needed them to be before you start becoming who you are meant to be.

CHAPTER FIVE
The Ransom for the Classroom

The road was eight miles of jagged gravel and relentless heat, and I walked it more often than most people would believe. On this particular morning, I had dressed with care—my elder sister's old brown skirt, hemmed by my own hand from the ankle to the knee, the stitches small and even, I was proud of my work. My brother Everton had helped me comb my hair, like all the other times before. I was feeling good. I was ready for school.

Hitchhiking was a common practice in rural Jamaica, not ideal but practical. If I could catch a free ride, I could save the few coins I had begged from my uncle Sikes for lunch. I was the only child in the neighborhood who seemed determined to show up on a Friday, and I stood at the bus stop alone—not afraid, just focused on the road and the opportunity it represented.

A beige Toyota Corolla slowed to a stop. The driver was clean-shaven, neatly dressed, and appeared to be a responsible adult. In Jamaica at that time, a man who could afford a Corolla was a man of some standing. I opened the door and asked politely if I could get a ride. “Yes, of course,” he said, and I climbed in with the easy trust of a girl who had been taught that politeness was its own kind of protection.

We talked about ordinary things for the first part of the journey—nothing specific, the easy surface conversation of strangers sharing a road. And then the air changed.

His questions shifted. His hand moved. The car became a cage.

“Do you have a boyfriend?” he asked. “No, Sir,” I said. “So no man has ever touched you—like this?” His hand reached toward me, and my heart became a frantic bird throwing itself against the bars of my ribs. I thought of my mother. I thought of how quickly a life could be taken on a Jamaican road. I started to plead. "Please, Sir. Don't. I won't tell anyone." I kept my voice low and steady, the way you speak to something dangerous, and I prayed.

"Please, Jesus. Please just let me get to school."

The neighboring town came into view, and I saw the clock tower—my landmark, my exit. "Sir, could you please drop me off at the clock?" He began to slow. Before the car came to a complete stop, I opened the door and jumped out onto the hot asphalt, the jagged gravel biting into the soles of my shoes, which were not my size.

I ran straight to my classroom, sat down, and opened my books. I told no one. Not that day, not for many years. I simply pressed the experience into the sealed vault where I kept all the things that threatened to break me, and I kept going. I held my schoolbook like a shield, and I kept going.

Education was the only ransom high enough to buy my freedom. Whatever the road demanded of me to reach that classroom, I would pay it. I had no other plan. I had no other option. And so I paid it, again and again, in ways that no child should ever have to pay.

###

End of Chapter Reflection Questions:

Pain is a passenger, but it should never be the driver.

Education is the only ransom that can buy your way out of a life defined by what was done to you. Is this a price worth paying? List the reasons why.

____

____

____

____

____

____

____

Pain is a passenger, but it should never be the driver. What pains are you currently allowing to steer your life?

____

____

____

____

____

Where have you kept silent about something that wounded you—and what might it cost you to continue that silence?

Architect's Blueprint:

The road to success is often patrolled by predators. Do not stop walking. Do not let them take your shield.

CHAPTER SIX
The Weight of Worlds

My sister Diana had made her own way to Boston, and that summer she invited me to come and spend a few months with her. I was seventeen years old, and America felt like a rumor that had finally agreed to be proven true.

Boston in the summer was a fever dream of red brick and possibility. The air smelled different—thick with a humidity that carried old paper and ambition instead of salt and roasted bananas. My sister's apartment was a temporary sanctuary, but the true cathedral I discovered was a bookstore downtown.

I had never seen so many pristine spines in one place. In Jamaica, books were precious, weathered things, passed from hand to hand until the edges curled like dried tobacco leaves. Not many people in my neighborhood could read well, and so there was little need for them. But here? Here were towers of untapped wisdom and gloss-coated dreams, floor to ceiling, aisle after aisle. I moved through them like a starving woman at a banquet.

My sister Diana would drop me off early and return hours later. I was in heaven. I wanted to inhale every word, claim every philosophy, own every story that promised a life beyond the horizon I knew. When the reality of the budget finally caught up with me, I chose with the precision of a surgeon—selecting each volume carefully, knowing that every dollar spent on a book was a dollar I would not regret.

By the time I packed for the flight home, my clothes were an afterthought shoved into the corners of my carry-on. My main suitcase was a leaden treasure chest, its zippers straining against the sheer density of paper and ink. It was the heaviest thing I had ever carried, and it felt like it gave me wings.

When I landed back in Jamaica, my brothers, Everton and Greg, were waiting with wide eyes and expectant grins. In our world, a suitcase from "foreign" meant new sneakers, toothpaste, electronics, or at the very least, the sweet processed crunch of American snacks. "Lord, look at the size of the bag!" Everton shouted. "What you bring for us, Mena?" Greg pressed, already circling the luggage like a hawk.

I unzipped the suitcase with a flush of pride.

Silence dropped over the room.

No bright plastics. No foreign things. Just the muted, matte covers of a dozen different worlds. My brothers reached in, their fingers brushing the heavy cardstock, and I watched the light vanish from their faces. For men who had struggled to string sentences into meaning, these pages were not gifts. They were a reminder of a door that remained locked to them.

"Books?" Greg whispered, his voice heavy with a disappointment that rivaled the weight of the bag itself. "You fill the whole grip with... paper?"

They walked away. We still laugh about it to this day.

But as I stacked those volumes on my small bedside table, their disappointment could not touch me. I opened a cover and felt the familiar pull of a world that made sense—where I was not just a girl from a big family in a small town, but a scholar, an explorer, a woman of means. To my brothers, life was what was happening in the dirt and the sun. To me, life was a draft I had the power to edit.

Between those covers, I built the first version of my 'Perfect Life.' It was not a fantasy. It was a rehearsal. And every woman who has ever visualized her way out of a situation she had no right to escape understands exactly what I mean.

###

End of Chapter Reflection Questions:

What is the difference between a 'need' and a 'sanctuary' in your own life? Have you ever had to defend a choice that others didn't understand but was vital to your growth?

____

____

____

____

____

____

____

When you look back at your journey, how has viewing your life as a story you were "architecting" helped you navigate the most difficult chapters without losing your sense of self?

____

____

____

____

____

____

____

Architect's Blueprint:

Imagination is your greatest ally. Do not lose sight of it.

CHAPTER SEVEN
The Double Witness

By the time I turned 19, I was beginning to feel the steady beat of my own independence. Life was no longer just about red dust and survival. It was about Saturday nights, plans with friends, the electric hum of a Valentine's party at the local skating rink. I had a job. I had a social life. For the first time, the future felt like it belonged entirely to me.

The road had one more lesson to teach me about who was actually at the wheel.

It was an ordinary Thursday morning when I boarded the bus called 'Pepper Seed'—a cramped, vibrant vehicle with its name stenciled on the front windshield, smelling of diesel and the press of bodies, windows down against the heat. I sat up front, tucked beside the driver, with two other passengers pressed against my left. The driver was a man in a hurry, treating the winding asphalt like a racetrack.

Somewhere through the journey, he took a corner too sharp and too fast. Time did not slow down; it shattered. The bus groaned—a sickening sound of metal surrendering to gravity—and we overturned once, twice, the world spinning into a blurred kaleidoscope of screams and breaking glass. When the motion finally stopped, the silence that followed was heavier than the bus itself.

I crawled out from the wreckage into a nightmare. People were pinned beneath the metal. There were fatalities that day. The damage was so severe that you could not even tell what color the bus had been. And I stood in the road and looked down at my body. Not a scratch. Not a bruise. Not a single drop of blood.

I took a taxi to my sister Margaret's house, the adrenaline finally giving way to a bone-deep tremor. I collapsed in her living room and looked toward the ceiling. "Jesus," I whispered, not in worship but in negotiation, the way you speak to someone you are not yet sure you trust. "If you were the one who saved my life, I want another proof."

The Lord did not make me wait.

The very next morning, I hitched another ride to work —because that was simply how things were done, and because I refused to let yesterday's terror become today's paralysis. We were not speeding. The road was straight. And then the earth seemed to shift again, the vehicle veering off and plunging into a ditch with a violent, metal-mangling crash. The car was destroyed. The driver and I walked away without a scratch.

Twice in twenty-four hours. Twice, completely unharmed.

I stood on the edge of that ditch with the dust settling around me, and I stopped asking for proof. "Ok, Lord," I whispered into the quiet morning air. "I now know it is You." I went back to Margaret's house, weeping and worshipping God.

I did not go to the Valentine's party that Saturday. On Sunday, I walked into the Pentecostal church in Bellfield—the same one that had stood in the gap for our family when our mother was killed, the one that had offered a hand when the world went gray. I did not walk to the altar. I ran.

I gave my life to the Lord and went down into the waters of baptism. Not long after, I was filled with the Holy Spirit and began speaking in new tongues. It was a fire that didn't consume—it clarified. It burned away the chaff and left only what was essential. Who I had known as Jesus, I would come to know more deeply over the years as Yeshua—the name I now hold most sacred, a reflection of a faith that has continued to grow and deepen through every season of my life.

He became the ultimate Architect of my 'After.' Not a distant figure in a book, but a Guide who had physically pulled me from wreckage twice to make certain I reached this moment. I give Him praise every single day. I may have paved the road. But he was the one who kept me from falling off the edge.

###

End of Chapter Reflection Questions:

Have there been moments in your life that defied every natural explanation? What would it mean for your future if you viewed those moments as divine intervention rather than luck?

____

____

____

____

____

____

____

How does the community that shows up during your darkest hour influence your long-term values? How can you be that sanctuary for someone else in their time of need?

____

____

____

____

____

____

____

Architect's Blueprint:

Nothing happens by accident. Every experience has led you to this day.

CHAPTER EIGHT
The End of the Beggar's Tongue

When Margaret was finally able to carve out her own space, she did not just leave the family home—she built a bridge and invited me to cross it. Moving from the chaotic, crowded world of our shared survival into the quiet sanctuary of her new household felt like stepping out of a storm and into a room where the windows had finally been shut against the wind.

For the first time in my life, the atmosphere of 'not enough' began to lift.

In the old house, survival was a loud and clashing thing—a constant negotiation with scarcity, every day a new calculation of who needed what most. But in Margaret's home, there was a revolutionary quiet. She had spent her teenage years being the shield for all of us, and now, in this new chapter, she turned that same fierce energy toward being my provider.

Before I moved in with her, I had mastered what I called the 'beggar scholar' persona. To get to school, to buy a pencil, to ensure a meal, I had become an expert in the art of the ask—tilting my head, softening my voice, calibrating my need to the mercy of whoever was in front of me. It was a daily, humiliating tax on my dignity that I paid without complaint because I had no alternative.

Under her roof, that tax was abolished.

I remember the first time I needed funds for a school project. My body braced automatically—heart tightening, words forming around the familiar shape of a plea. Before I could finish the sentence, she reached into her purse and handed me what I needed. No lecture. No weight placed on the gift. No making me feel the smallness of having to ask. "Go to your lessons, Mena," she said, her voice steady as an anchor. "The books are your only job right now."

For the first time in my life, I was allowed to simply be a student.

Margaret worked with a focused, relentless grace that I watched with wide-eyed wonder. She ensured my uniforms were clean and pressed, my stomach was full, and my tuition was a priority above all else. My hitchhiking days were over. She was the one who taught me that a woman's hands could do more than hold things together—they could build a world where the next generation didn't have to beg.

Living with her was my first real taste of the "Perfect Life" I had previously only found in the pages of my books. Not physical luxury—we were far from that. But the luxury of certainty. The luxury of waking up and knowing that today, I would be taken care of. That was the richest I had ever been.

Margaret became the blueprint for the executive I would eventually become. She showed me that true leadership is not about giving orders. It is about providing the resources so that those under your care can finally stop looking at the ground and start looking at the horizon.

###

End of Chapter Reflection Questions:

How did the removal of daily humiliation open your mind to higher goals? How can you create environments—in your home, your business, your community—that protect people's dignity while they grow?

____
____
____
____
____
____
____

Who were the 'bridge-builders' in your early life? In what specific ways are you currently acting as a bridge for those who are still walking the red dust paths you once traveled?

____
____
____
____
____

Architect's Blueprint:

Bridges are built to cross. Don't be afraid, cross them.

CHAPTER NINE

The Three-Bus Redemption

America was the land of the 4:00 AM alarm.

I had arrived at twenty-six years old—full of ambition, met at the airport by my eldest sister Margaret, who had made the crossing before me and built a small, sturdy foothold in this new world. Opportunity and family had pulled me across the ocean, and I arrived believing that all the hard work was behind me. I did not yet understand that the American chapter of my life would ask just as much of me as Jamaica had—it would simply ask it in a different language.

My life in those early years was measured in bus transfers. Three buses to work, three buses home.

That is thirty buses a week, one hundred and twenty buses a month, and one thousand four hundred and forty buses a year—numbers I calculated in my head on those long rides, not out of despair but out of habit, the way a woman who has always had to count every resource counts everything.

One particular morning was the hardest. I walked to the daycare at five in the morning, pushing a stroller I had found on the side of the road, its wheels hanging at a compromised angle, eight-year-old Candice bundled inside. The rain hit my face, and I could not tell the difference between the rainwater and the tears. I could not afford to miss the bus. I could not afford to lose my job. I could not afford, in any sense of the word, to stop.

What I did not tell anyone during those years—what I barely admitted to myself—was that I was also taking classes. I had enrolled to pursue my MBA while working full time and raising my daughter alone, because I understood something I had learned in Jamaica at the feet of my sister Margaret: the only way out is through education, and the only way through education is to decide that no circumstance will stop you from reaching it. I was building my future on the bus, in the margins of textbooks, in the stolen quiet of a sleeping child.

But the weight of those years was not only physical. It was emotional, and it had a name: resentment.

I had found a way, without meaning to, to blame my mother for all of it. For the three buses. For the stroller with the broken wheels. For the rain. My anger at her—the nine-year-old's fury at a woman who had "allowed herself" to be murdered—had calcified over the years into something harder and more useful. It kept me moving. It kept me from feeling too much. And it expressed itself in the strangest way: I forbade Mother's Day.

I refused Candice's words, her cards, her flowers, her handmade construction paper offerings. I would quietly discard them, unable to hold them without feeling the void they were meant to fill. I was punishing the present for the sins of the past. I was protecting my heart, but I was starving my daughter's.

"How could you allow yourself to be murdered?" was the prayer I kept alive in the private chambers of my heart. "I will never forgive you for this." The anger kept me upright when grief might have leveled me. But it also kept me from fully receiving the love that was being offered to me by the little girl who had done nothing wrong.

It took me many years to see it clearly. About five years ago, I finally did. I looked at what I was doing—the cards I had thrown away, the celebrations I had refused, the distance I had maintained from the one person who loved me most—and I recognized it for what it was: I was letting my past reach forward and damage my present. I was letting a ghost make decisions for a living woman.

I let it go. Not all at once, and not without grief. But I let it go.

On the next Mother's Day, I held the flowers my daughter brought me and did not throw them away.

###

End of Chapter Reflection Questions:

Resentment is a wall you build to keep out pain, but eventually, it keeps out the love.

What celebrations are you avoiding because a ghost is still haunting you?

Are you ready to let that ghost go? Why, or why not?

Where in your life are you letting the past make decisions that belong to the present?

Architect's Blueprint:

Resentment is a debt you try to collect from a person who has no money. Cancel the debt so you can finally be rich in love.

CHAPTER TEN
The Annual Mourning

While my other siblings and I carried the jagged shards of memory—the sound of our mother's laughter, the specific way she tucked us in, the scent of her skin—my youngest brother Greg carried something much heavier: an empty space.

He was three years old when his world went gray. At three, your mother is the sun around which your entire universe orbits. When that sun was extinguished, he had no words for the darkness. He simply learned to live in the shadows. I watched him grow—a quiet boy moving through a house of grieving giants—and my heart would ache with a specific, helpless kind of sorrow.

I could remember our mother vaguely. The smells, mostly spaghetti and meatballs she had learned to cook during a visit to Canada, the particular warmth of her presence in a room. Greg remembered only the longing. A shape without a face. A warmth he had never been able to name.

The true depth of that hollow space did not reveal itself in childhood. It waited for the milestones of adulthood to demand its due. Every year, when the calendar turns to the second Sunday of May, my phone would ring. I did not need to look at the caller ID.

"Mena," he will whisper, his voice thick with a grief that time has refused to heal. "Tell me about her again. Tell me what she sounded like. Tell me if I have her eyes. Tell me why I do not have a mother."

In those moments, I am no longer just his sister. I am the keeper of the flame. I reach back into my vault of memory and pull out whatever colors I can find—the specific details that make a ghost into a woman—and I paint a picture for a man who has lived his entire life in black and white. He is mourning someone he never got to know, a presence that exists for him only in the stories we tell.

The impact of that missing piece has been the invisible architect of his entire life. Without the primary blueprint of a mother's love, he navigated the world with a compass that never quite found north. He struggled with belonging. With a low-grade fever of "not being enough" that no external success could fully soothe.

My brother never knew about my private resentment toward our mother. He never knew that I was punishing her in my own way, forbidding her memory from taking up space in the present. I maintained the keeper of the flame role without ever letting him see the fire that burned inside me alongside it. I pretended. And while I did it to protect him, I understand now that pretending is not a gift—it is a delay. It postpones the healing that can only happen when we are willing to confront what is true.

Watching Greg cry as an adult has been one of the most instructive experiences of my life. It reminds me that the Architect's work is never finished. We do not just build for ourselves. We build to fill the gaps for those who will come after us, those who were too young to lay their own foundations. My mission—my "After"—is not only about my own pain. It is about being the bridge of memory for my brother, ensuring that even if he never knew her touch, he will always know her worth.

###

End of Chapter Reflection Questions:

How does 'grieving a memory' differ from 'grieving an absence'? How do you support someone who is struggling with a void they cannot name?

What stories or legacies in your family or community are you responsible for preserving? How does sharing those 'vibrant colors' help heal the gray-scale wounds of others?

____
____
____
____
____
____
____

Architect's Blueprint:

Pretending does not bring healing.

Confronting your emotions does.

CHAPTER ELEVEN
The Shared Silence

In the aftermath of 1981, our house didn't just hold six children. It held six different versions of a shipwreck. We were all tossed into the same violent sea, but each of us grabbed for a different piece of driftwood to stay afloat. Grief is not a monolithic weight. It is a prism that refracts through the personality of the bereaved, turning the same loss into six distinct shades of survival.

Margaret, the Teen Matriarch, chose Fortification. Her grief became a cold, hard stone she used to build a wall around the rest of us. She didn't have the luxury of tears; they would have blurred her vision, and she needed to see every threat clearly. For her, mourning was a currency she traded for groceries, laundry, and the quiet, fierce discipline of our survival.

One of my brothers chose Combustion. His grief was a fire that burned through the red dirt of the neighborhood. He became restless, angry, and quick to challenge a world that had proven it could be cruel without consequence. His pain was a scream that no one wanted to hear, so he turned it into a fist.

Then there was the Quiet Observer. Another brother seemed to fold into the shadows of the house, becoming as still as the furniture. He didn't fight, and he didn't lead. He simply waited, watching the palms grow from the red soil with an eerie detachment, as though waiting for the earth to offer an explanation that never came.

And then there was me. I chose Imagination.

While my brothers were fighting or fading, I was building. I took the gray-scale struggle and ran it through the filter of books, of dreaming, of the "Perfect Life" I rehearsed in the quiet of my mind. I could not change the beginning of the story. But I was determined to be the one who designed the After.

Despite our different maps, we all ended up in the same territory of silence. We rarely spoke of that day—not in childhood, not even in adulthood. We moved around the void at the center of our lives as if it were a piece of high-voltage equipment: dangerous to touch, impossible to ignore. We built our separate structures on the same volatile ground. Some built fortresses. Some built fires. Some built nothing at all and waited for the ground to tell them what to do.

But looking at my siblings now, I see the truth clearly: the Architect doesn't build only one way. Sometimes you build a fortress. Sometimes you build a fire. Sometimes you build in the silence of your own imagination, brick by invisible brick, until the day you walk out into the light and realize you have been building something real all along.

As long as you are building, the soil has not won.

###

End of Chapter Reflection Questions:

When you look at the people in your life—colleagues, clients, family—how does understanding that everyone processes shipwrecks differently help you lead with more empathy and less judgment?

____
____
____
____
____
____
____

Which path do you naturally lean toward during a crisis: Fortification, Combustion, Detachment, or Imagination? Is that path still serving the person you have become?

____
____
____
____
____
____
____
____

Architect's Blueprint:

The same storm produces different structures. The measure is not how you grieve. It is that you keep building.

CHAPTER TWELVE
The Hurricane

It was 2005 when a hurricane stripped away my home. The world called it Katrina.

I had made all the necessary preparations, monitoring every news station with the focused calm of a woman who had survived Jamaican storms before. I was living in a two-bedroom apartment on the second floor, and Candice—eight years old—was with me. When the wind began in earnest, I could hear the neighbors scurrying like rats to make last-minute preparations they should have made days earlier. Candice and I were playing a game, pretending the ordinary could hold against the extraordinary.

Then I heard it: the booming percussion of trees falling on the apartment roof. Through the slats of the blinds, I watched the neighbor's roof across the street lift off like the lid of a pot. I had experienced a hurricane of this magnitude once before—Gilbert, when I was fifteen and living with Margaret in Coopers Penn, Jamaica, the worst storm the island had seen in my lifetime. The difference between then and now was simple and terrifying: this time, I was alone with my daughter.

An eerie quietness descended, sudden and absolute. I knew what it meant—the eye of the storm, the most deceptive moment, the pause that makes people believe it is over. I watched through the blinds as neighbors stepped outside to assess the damage. Then the great wind returned with a sound like the earth clearing its throat, and people began rushing back inside. I grabbed Candice and ran to the bathroom, hovering over her, praying with everything I had.

Eventually, the storm passed. I walked gingerly into the living room and felt water on my face. I looked up. There was a hole in the ceiling large enough to see the sky. Water gushed in furiously, soaking the carpet, claiming the living room as its own. The bedrooms, miraculously, were intact. I pried the swollen front door open and stepped outside. My car was undamaged. I exhaled for what felt like the first time in hours.

We spent that night in the apartment, and then many nights after. Eventually, the authorities condemned the building as uninhabitable.

With nowhere else to go, I did what I had always done: I kept moving. Candice and I lived out of the car — professional by day, homeless mother by night. I dressed for work in the backseat, and helped Candice choose her clothes for school from plastic bags tucked in the trunk, each selection made with the quiet precision of a woman who refused to let her circumstances announce themselves. I never shed a tear in Candice's presence. She did not need to carry what I was carrying.

One evening, I was digging through those bags looking for a silk blouse, and the sound of the rain on the car roof—closer, more insistent than the hurricane wind had been on the apartment ceiling—broke something open in me. Not in despair, but in decision.

"Enough," I said to no one in particular, and I meant it with every cell in my body. This was not the life I had crossed an ocean to build.

I reached out to the Red Cross. Within weeks, I used the assistance I received as a down payment on a townhouse.

The storm did not define me. The decision I made in its aftermath did.

###

End of Chapter Reflection Questions:

You are not defined by where you sleep tonight. You are defined by where you are headed tomorrow.

How do the storms in your life—literal or metaphorical—give you the resolve to make decisions you might otherwise avoid?

____

____

____

What is the difference between fleeing a tragedy and intentionally driving toward a different destination? What are you doing right now?

Architect's Blueprint:

A roof is just wood and shingles. Your real shelter is the resolve inside your bones.

CHAPTER THIRTEEN
The Policy of Presence

Success had finally arrived—the mahogany desk, the title of Insurance Professional, the crisp ozone scent of a laser printer, and a life I had built from nothing. After 16 years in claims, I had heard the call to serve people in a deeper way. I had watched too many families discover—in their worst moments—that they did not understand what they actually had, or what they were missing. I wanted to change that. In 2024, I made the leap and opened my own agency. I was now the woman who helped people protect what mattered most.

The irony of what came next is not lost on me.

It was a routine mammogram—the kind of appointment a responsible woman keeps on the calendar the way she keeps oil changes and annual reviews, with the quiet confidence that the results will confirm what she already knows: that she is fine. The technician noted that the lines were not straight. That sentence, delivered so clinically, so matter-of-factly, was the beginning of a conversation that would reorder everything.

It was a Friday afternoon at approximately 4:30 when I saw my doctor's number appear on my cell phone. Three days had passed since the follow-up tests. Everyone knows what they say: if your doctor hasn't called within three days, you're fine. I answered with the easy confidence of a woman who had survived hurricanes, three-bus mornings, and a childhood that should have broken her.

"Mena, it's not good news."

I asked her to repeat herself. I asked if she was certain those were my results. She said yes. She asked me to come in first thing Monday morning. I set the phone down on the mahogany desk and looked at the photographs on my office wall—the degrees, the designations, the evidence of every mile I had walked. They could not save me from this. No credential, no title, no polished stillness could stand between me and what the scan had revealed.

And then something ancient and certain rose up from somewhere deep inside me.

I went home. I found a quiet place. And I laid face down before the Lord.

I did not bargain. I did not perform. I simply prostrated myself before the One who had pulled me from two wrecked vehicles and kept me intact through a Category 5 hurricane, and I said, in the language that has no words: "I trust You." When I rose from that floor, I knew—with a certainty that had nothing to do with medicine and everything to do with the God I had walked with since a young woman ran to the altar in Bellfield—that it was going to be alright.

Early detection. No chemotherapy. No radiation. Hormone treatment, and the steady, unglamorous work of healing. Donovan was there—present in the most practical and profound of ways, measuring fluids from my drains, helping me to the bathroom, performing with quiet tenderness the functions I could not perform for myself. My sisters were there. My closest friends were there. The community I had spent a lifetime building showed up in the way that true community does: not with grand gestures, but with presence.

Luna was there too.

She is not the kind of companion I ever imagined needing. I did not grow up with dogs in the house—in Jamaica, that is simply not what we did, and I had carried that cultural preference with me across the ocean without question. But Donovan has always loved dogs, always wanted one, and somewhere along the way, I gave in.

And in those weeks of medical leave, Luna made me understand why.

She would sit outside the bathroom door and wait—patient, still, and completely unbothered by the inconvenience of devotion—until I emerged. She followed me from room to room as though she had been assigned to me, her warm weight settling beside me wherever I landed. She did not need me to explain what was happening or pretend that everything was fine. She simply stayed. In the quiet language of a creature who asks for nothing but your presence, she kept me company through every slow and tender day of my recovery.

I have never been a dog person. But Luna is not just a dog. She is family. And when the world grew very still and the days were long, and the healing was slow... She was exactly what I did not know I needed. Proof that sometimes, love arrives on four legs, parks itself outside your bathroom door, and refuses to leave until you are whole.

The policy of presence—the thing I had been selling to clients for years, the assurance that someone would show up in the moment of greatest need—was now being honored in my own life.

What that experience changed in me is not dramatic. It is quiet and permanent. It made me more compassionate—not the surface compassion of someone who says the right things, but the bone-deep kind that comes from having needed people and having had them arrive. It deepened my faith in ways that prosperity had not and could not. And it reminded me, with a force that no motivational phrase has ever matched, that the life I am living is not a guarantee. It is a gift, and the only fitting response to such a gift is to remain entirely and purposefully present within each moment.

I am not the woman who was told the news in that office anymore. I am the woman who got up off the floor.

###

End of Chapter Reflection Questions:

Security is not the absence of danger. It is the presence of peace.

Where in your life are you insuring everyone else's future while neglecting your own? What would it mean to finally apply the "policy of presence" to yourself?

____

____

____

____

____

____

____

When was the last time you truly surrendered a fear —not suppressed it, but released it? What did that feel like, and what became possible on the other side?

Who shows up for you? And are you allowing them to?

Architect's Blueprint:

Security is not the absence of risk. It is the presence of peace. Are you insuring your life, or are you living it?

CHAPTER FOURTEEN
The Red Soil Return

The journey back was never just about miles. It was about the decades of avoidance I was finally willing to end.

When I stepped out of the car and stood in the old neighborhood, the silence was heavy and familiar, broken only by the dry whistle of wind through cane stalks. I stood by that crumbling concrete wall—the silent witness to the day my world fractured in January of 1981—and looked down at my feet.

Red dust, fine as cinnamon and persistent as memory, had already begun to settle on the polished leather of my shoes. In any other setting, I would have reached for a cloth. Here, the stain felt like an overdue conversation.

For years, I had viewed this earth with a shuddering breath. I thought the red dirt was a thief. I believed it had swallowed my mother's vibrant, living essence and left me with nothing but a gray-scale hunger for a life I couldn't yet name. I thought the soil was a grave.

I was wrong.

I looked up from my feet to the towering trees swaying above me, their leaves a deep and defiant green against a sky so blue it hurt. They were drinking from the same earth I had feared. Their roots were buried deep in the very red dirt I had spent decades trying to escape. And they were magnificent.

The revelation arrived with the force of a tropical storm: I had not been buried. I had been planted.

The tragedy was not an ending. It was an agricultural necessity. To grow something as unyielding as the woman I had become, the seed had to be placed in the dark. The red soil was not my enemy. It was the mineral-rich foundation of my entire architecture—providing the harsh and necessary nutrients of resilience, forcing me upward, demanding that I break through the surface and reach for a sun that my ancestors had only glimpsed through the bars of their own struggles.

I reached down and touched the earth. I let the grit move between my fingers.

And in that gesture, I finally stopped the silent, internal trial in which I had been prosecuting my mother for thirty-plus years. I stopped seeing her death as abandonment and started seeing her life as the ultimate act of a gardener—a woman who gave what she had so that something could grow from it. I am the fruit of that planting. Bitter at first, perhaps. But ripe now, with a success that feeds more than just my own ambitions.

I looked at the wall one last time. It was no longer a monument to murder. It was a marker of a beginning.

If you find yourself in the dark, pressed down by the weight of a world that feels like it is closing in, do not panic. Do not mistake the shadows for the end of the story.

You are a seed. And the dirt is just the place where your After begins to take root.

###

End of Chapter Reflection Questions:

What soil in your life have you been treating as a grave, when it might actually be the ground for your greatest growth?

____
____
____
____
____
____
____

What would change in how you see your past if you reframed every hard season as preparation rather than punishment?

____
____
____
____
____

____

____

____

What does returning to your "red soil"—the place, the person, or the memory you have been avoiding—hold for you?

____

____

____

____

____

____

____

Architect's Blueprint:

Don't mistake the dirt for the end. The darker the soil, the stronger the roots.

CHAPTER FIFTEEN
The Sovereign Seat

The engine of the Mercedes-Benz hums with a low, expensive vibration—a sound that does not just indicate power, but peace. I sit in the driver's seat, feeling the cool, buttery embrace of the leather against my skin. The air conditioner breathes a steady, mountain-chill frost into the cabin, a stark contrast to the thick, suffocating heat of the neighborhood streets I once navigated on foot.

Through the windshield, the silver hood emblem catches the afternoon sun. It does not just point toward the road; it points toward a horizon I mapped, surveyed, and paved with my own hands. For decades, I was a passenger in a life driven by circumstance, tragedy, and the needs of others. Today, my hands are steady on the wheel.

The door opens. Candice steps in, bringing with her the spicy-sweet perfume of roses—red petals waxen and perfect, standing tall against emerald stems. In another life, flowers were for funerals. They were the scent of the gray-scale days after 1981, the olfactory trigger for everything I had refused to feel. But as I pull my daughter close and bury my face in the blooms, the ghosts do not materialize. Instead, I feel the weight of a legacy—the solid, unbreakable reality of a woman who turned a ransom into a fortune.

"I'm celebrating the Architect," she whispers against my shoulder.

The roses are not an offering for what was lost. They are a coronation for what has been built.

I think about the road that led here. The red dust. The eight-mile walk in a hemmed-up skirt. The classroom that became my sanctuary. The Boston bookstore that became my first university. The altar in Bellfield, where I ran and did not walk. The bus transfers, the stroller with the broken wheel, the MBA I pursued from the backseat of a car that held everything I owned. The floor where I prostrated myself before the Lord and rose up knowing it would be alright. The red soil I finally touched with open hands.

My faith has grown with me through every season—from the Pentecostal church in Jamaica that stood in the gap when my mother was taken, through the Spirit-filled communities of my early American years, and into the Messianic Jewish faith I now hold as my own. Each chapter of my spiritual journey has deepened my understanding of the God who kept pulling me from wreckage and placing me back on solid ground. He has been the ultimate Architect of my After, and I give Him praise every day.

I am not the girl in the red dust anymore. That child—with her grit and her books and her stubborn, unassailable refusal to become the victim the world wanted to make her—was the apprentice. She did the heavy lifting so that the woman I am today could hold the title.

I have traded the weight of a suitcase full of books for the weight of a life full of purpose. I have moved from the roadside to the executive suite, from the backseat of a car in the dark to the sovereign seat I now occupy with intention and with gratitude.

I am Mena. I am Dr. Nalhlie Daly. I am the Architect.

And the road ahead? That belongs to me.

Now it is your turn.

You are holding the keys. The engine is running. The tank is full of every hard-won lesson, every mile of red dust, every moment of grace that has brought you to this page. The blueprints have been drawn. The foundation has been laid.

Where will you build first?

###

End of Chapter Reflection Questions:

What does your "Sovereign Seat" look like? Describe it in as much detail as you can—who is there, what surrounds you, what does it feel like to finally be in it?

What is one decision you have been delaying that the Architect inside you already knows is the right one?

What is your 'After,' and what is the first brick you will lay to begin building it today?

Architect's Blueprint:

You are holding the keys. You are the Architect of your After.

THE ARCHITECT'S AFFIRMATIONS

Speak these over yourself. Speak them even when you do not yet believe them.

I am not the dirt that held me; I am the life that broke through it.

My 'After' is not a destination; it is a masterpiece of my own design.

I hold the keys to the vehicle of my life. I decide who sits in the passenger seat.

I was not buried. I was planted. And I will bloom in every season.

The road behind me proves I was built for the road ahead.

I do not wait to be rescued. I am the rescue.

Every storm I have survived has made my foundation stronger.

I forgive not because I am weak, but because I refuse to be a prisoner of someone else's choices.

I am the Architect. I design my own After.

The End.

About the Author

The Architect

Nalhlie Daly, Hon. Dr., was born and raised in Jamaica, West Indies, and now calls Henry County, Georgia, home. An Insurance Agent with over sixteen years of prior leadership experience in corporate operations, she built her professional life the same way she built everything else — one intentional decision at a time.

But Dr. Daly's reach extends far beyond the walls of her agency. In Henry County, she is known as a force for community transformation. She has championed fire safety awareness alongside the local Fire Department, delivered educational presentations in schools, organized back-to-school donation drives, and provided backpacks filled with food for children facing food insecurity. She has sponsored local school teams, participated in career days, supported veterans' events, and mentored young entrepreneurs on the twin pillars of ambition and responsibility.

Her civic fingerprints are visible throughout the county. She has supported the Civic Bee Competition and Leadership Henry – programs designed to cultivate informed, engaged, and capable community members – and has actively been involved with the Henry County Chamber of Commerce and the JAICC. She has been featured in print publications, invited to speak on the role of insurance and financial preparedness, and interviewed on radio platforms that reach the audiences she most wants to serve.

Dr. Daly holds an Honorary Doctorate in Humanities, a Master of Business Administration with a concentration in Accounting and Finance, and a Bachelor of Business Administration. She carries professional designations as a Chartered Financial

Consultant, Chartered Property and Casualty Underwriter, and Chartered Life Underwriter, along with several securities licenses and a Certified Life Coach credential. Her education and her lived experience are not separate chapters — they are the same story told in two languages.

She is married to Donovan and is the proud mother of her daughter, Candice, and their dog, Luna. When she is not building community or serving clients, she can be found traveling to new places, losing herself in a good book, or in the middle of a workout she is absolutely going to finish.

She has been the girl on the shoulder of the road. Now she is the Architect.

www.ingramcontent.com/pod-product-compliance
Lightning Source LLC
LaVergne TN
LVHW090614110826
845146LV00001B/380

* 9 7 9 8 9 9 6 0 8 6 9 0 0 *